THE LOUISIANA PURCHASE

by Rebecca Rowell

Content Consultant
David Peterson Del Mar
Associate Professor, Department of History
Portland State University

Core Library

An Imprint of Abdo Publishing
abdopublishing.com

abdopublishing.com

Published by Abdo Publishing, a division of ABDO, PO Box 398166, Minneapolis, Minnesota 55439. Copyright © 2017 by Abdo Consulting Group, Inc. International copyrights reserved in all countries. No part of this book may be reproduced in any form without written permission from the publisher. Core Library™ is a trademark and logo of Abdo Publishing.

Printed in the United States of America, North Mankato, Minnesota
042016
092016

Cover Photo: Everett Historical/Shutterstock Images
Interior Photos: Everett Historical/Shutterstock Images, 1; SuperStock/Glow Images, 4, 16; Red Line Editorial, 7, 21, 40; Bettmann/Corbis, 9, 34; Edgar Samuel Paxson (1852–1915)/Private Collection/Peter Newark American Pictures/Bridgeman Images, 12; Corbis, 18; Lehman & Duval Lithrs./Library of Congress, 24, 45; North Wind Picture Archives, 28; Hulton Archive/Getty Images, 31; Terry Ashe/AP Images, 38

Editor: Marie Pearson
Series Designer: Ryan Gale

Cataloging-in-Publication Data
Names: Rowell, Rebecca, author.
Title: The Louisiana Purchase / by Rebecca Rowell.
Description: Minneapolis, MN : Abdo Publishing, [2017] | Series: The wild West
    | Includes bibliographical references and index.
Identifiers: LCCN 2015960521 | ISBN 9781680782561 (lib. bdg.) |
    ISBN 9781680776676 (ebook)
Subjects: LCSH: Louisiana Purchase--Juvenile literature. | United States--
    Territorial expansion--Juvenile literature. | Frontier and pioneer life ((U.S.)--
    Juvenile literature.
Classification: DDC 973.4--dc23
LC record available at http://lccn.loc.gov/2015960521

CONTENTS

AN IRRESISTIBLE OFFER

The United States and France made a historic agreement in 1803. The United States purchased 529,920,000 acres (214,450,000 ha) of land in North America. The territory stretched from the Mississippi River to the Rocky Mountains. It ran from the Gulf of Mexico to Canada. It was larger than France, Germany, the United Kingdom, Italy, Portugal, and Spain combined. It was known as the

Thomas Jefferson was president at the time of the purchase. He wanted the United States to expand west.

A Brief History of the Territory

French explorer Robert Cavelier claimed the Mississippi River Basin for France in 1682. He named the area Louisiana after French king Louis XIV. In 1718 another French explorer, Jean-Baptiste le Moyne, settled nearby. He founded Nouvelle Orléans, or New Orleans. By the mid-1700s, France controlled more of what is now the United States than any other European power. France gave Spain some land west of the Mississippi River in 1762. It was called French Louisiana. Spain did little with the territory. In 1801 Spain returned the land to France.

Louisiana Territory. And on May 2, US and French officials made it final. They signed the Louisiana Purchase treaty.

Making an Offer

The deal started with President Thomas Jefferson. He was interested in New Orleans. The city was on the mouth of the Mississippi River. France controlled the city. France also owned the Louisiana Territory. The river was vital to many Americans. Developing cities relied on it for

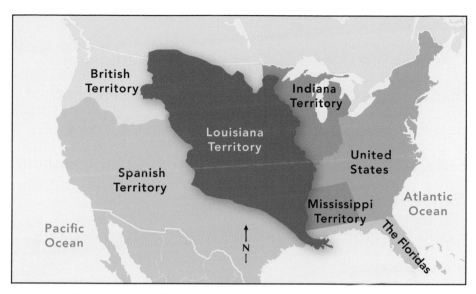

Territories of 1803

Study this map of the United States and its neighboring territories in 1803. What is different from the United States today? What is the same?

moving supplies and merchandise. Farmers used it to sell their goods.

When Jefferson took office in 1801, one of his top goals was to get control of the city. He gave Robert Livingston the task of negotiating a deal. Livingston was the US minister to France. Livingston was to offer France $2 million to buy the city, parts of the Mississippi's east bank, and free access to the river for business purposes. But news reached Jefferson that Americans could no longer ship goods from New

Orleans. The United States needed the area more than ever. Jefferson sent James Monroe, who had previously been the US minister to France, to help Livingston. Jefferson authorized up to $10 million for the port of New Orleans and the Floridas. The Floridas were parts of present-day Florida, Alabama, and Mississippi.

Napoléon Bonaparte, France's leader, had plans for the region. He wanted to create an empire in the New World. But he ran into trouble in the Caribbean. In 1801 Napoléon sent troops to France's colony on the island of Hispaniola. That was present-day Dominican Republic and Haiti. The troops fought a slave uprising. More than 40,000 French soldiers died during ten months of fighting. France lost the fight. It was the most successful slave revolution in history. This ruined Napoléon's hopes for a French empire in the Americas.

Now Napoléon needed money for a war with the United Kingdom. So he offered the entire

Livingstone (*center*) and Monroe (*right*) agreed to buy the whole territory.

Louisiana Territory to the United States. He asked for just $15 million. The move shocked Livingston and Monroe. The amount was more than Jefferson had approved the men to spend. It was more than the United States could afford. But they had to take the offer. It was too good to refuse. The United States borrowed money from European banks and made the purchase.

Federalist Opposition

Most Federalists were against the Louisiana Purchase. The Federalist Party was largely centered in New England. Buying the Louisiana Territory meant the South might gain more power than the Federalists. Federalist Fisher Ames wrote in protest, "We are to give money of which we have too little for land of which we already have too much." Only one Federalist was for the purchase. The Senate approved the purchase on October 20, 1803. The vote was 24 to 7.

What It Meant

The Louisiana Purchase marked change for America. The exchange of land was by choice, not by force. Countries usually fight for land. These nations made the deal voluntarily. And the deal doubled the size of the country. The United States became one of the world's largest nations.

But settling the West presented challenges. Native Americans inhabited the territory.

The US government sought to gain control of their lands.

Slavery also became an important issue. At the time of the Louisiana Purchase, the practice was legal in much of the United States. Debates raged between supporters of slavery and opponents, or abolitionists. People argued whether slavery should be allowed in the vast new frontier. The slavery debate and the treatment of Native Americans in the West would become two of the most tragic legacies of the 1800s.

FURTHER EVIDENCE

Chapter One covers events leading to the Louisiana Purchase. What is one of the main points of the chapter? What evidence supports this point? Visit the website below and find a quote that supports the main point in this chapter. Does the quote support an existing piece of evidence in the chapter? Or does it add a new one?

Thomas Jefferson's Monticello: Louisiana Purchase

mycorelibrary.com/louisiana-purchase

CHAPTER TWO

EXPLORING THE LAND

Thomas Jefferson was eager to explore the West. He arranged an expedition even before the Louisiana Purchase. He wanted a team to explore the Missouri River and meet with Native Americans. They were to broaden the American fur trade and search for a northwest passage to the Pacific Ocean. Now the territory was in their possession. The trip was even more important. The explorers would investigate

Meriwether Lewis (left) and William Clark (middle) explored the new land with the help of Sacagawea, their translator.

the country's new land. They would look for areas that promised agricultural and commercial success.

Lewis and Clark

Jefferson's personal secretary, Meriwether Lewis, would head the expedition. Lewis asked William Clark to be co-commander. The two men had served together in the military.

Lewis and Clark set out from Saint Louis, Missouri, on May 14, 1804. They headed for the Pacific Northwest. They were accompanied by approximately 50 men. They were called the Corps of Discovery. They planned to trek northwest to the Pacific Ocean. The journey was almost 8,000 miles (13,000 km).

Lewis recorded information Jefferson requested. This would tell Jefferson of ways to profit from the land. Lewis noted latitude and longitude. He described the climate, soil, plants, and animals. He made notes about meetings with Native Americans.

Jefferson wanted the team to act as diplomats with the Native Americans. They were to create friendly ties with tribes. So the Corps held military parades. They gave flags, peace medals, and other gifts. These included metal pots and corn mills. Some items were meant to show how the white settlers had better technology. Others were meant to inspire tribes to give up their hunting way of life for farming. Farming would require less land. Jefferson believed this would encourage tribes to give up their lands to the United States.

Lewis and his men gave speeches. They promised trade and asked for peace among the tribes. Most Native Americans the Corps encountered were friendly.

PERSPECTIVES
Spain's Concern

The Spanish were concerned about the United States' western expeditions. If Lewis and Clark found a northwest passage to the Pacific Ocean, the United States might try to take Spanish territory in the Southwest. The Spanish did not like that idea. The Southwest was rich in gold. The governor of New Mexico, a Spanish territory, sent soldiers to capture the expedition. But the soldiers failed. The Spanish simply could not find the explorers.

The Shoshone and several other Native American nations helped Lewis and Clark's expedition.

They were happy to trade with the men. They gave the men food, shelter, information, entertainment, and even tribe members to act as guides. They sometimes helped in exchange for guns.

The Corps spent its first winter in North Dakota, near present-day Bismarck. They built and stayed at Fort Mandan. Lewis and Clark readied items for Jefferson. These included maps and samples of animals, plants, and minerals. On April 7, 1805, Lewis and Clark sent a few of their men back to Saint Louis with the shipment. The rest of the party continued west.

The team joyfully reached the Pacific Ocean in November 1805. They stayed near present-day Astoria, Oregon, for the winter. They built Fort Clatsop. Team members dried meat, made salt, and wrote in their journals.

The Fur Trade

Lewis and Clark described the Upper Missouri Region, now Montana, the Dakotas, Minnesota, and Iowa, as having many beavers and bison but few trading posts. After their notes were published, trade in the area grew. Trade centered on bison robes. And trade rose rapidly. The American Fur Company shipped 40,000 furs a year in the 1830s. By the 1850s, they were shipping 100,000 a year. Native Americans traded furs for goods. These included coffee, tobacco, fabric, knives, spoons, and tin cups.

Pike was an army officer as well as an explorer.

The group started their return journey when the snow melted.

The Corps arrived in Saint Louis on September 23, 1806. They did not find a northwest passage or create a fur trade in the West. But they met members of almost 50 Native American tribes. They also gathered important information about the land. Lewis recorded new wildlife, including 122 animals and 178 plants.

Pike Expedition

The Corps of Discovery was not the only Louisiana Territory expedition. Jefferson appointed James Wilkinson, a former army general, as governor of the territory. Wilkinson tasked Zebulon Pike with exploring the territory. On August 9, 1805, Pike traveled north. He was searching for the source of the Mississippi River. Pike and 20 other men traveled by boat and foot from Saint Louis, Missouri, to northern Minnesota. The trip was 2,000 miles (3,200 km).

Pike mistakenly determined Leech Lake as the source of the Mississippi. But he did negotiate a treaty with leaders of a Dakota tribe in present-day Minnesota. The government had not given him that power. Even so, he offered the tribe $200 worth of items. In exchange, the United States gained access to land that is now part of Minneapolis and St. Paul for military use. In the treaty, Pike promised $200,000 to the tribe. The US government paid only $2,000. Pike returned to Saint Louis on April 30, 1806.

In 1806, Wilkinson sent Pike west on another mission. This time, Pike would explore the Arkansas and Red Rivers. He was to learn about the Spanish Territory. That region was west of the Louisiana Territory. But the Spanish captured Pike. They charged him with entering New Mexico illegally. They released Pike and his team in Natchitoches, Louisiana Territory, on June 30, 1807.

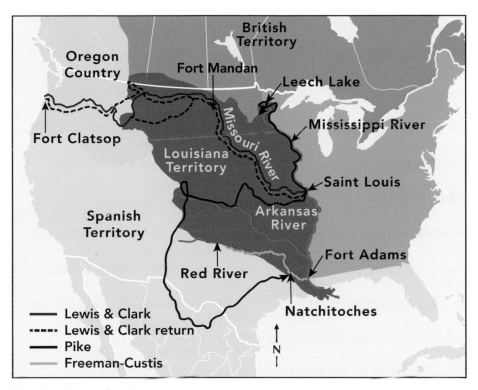

British Territory

Oregon Country

Fort Mandan

Leech Lake

Mississippi River

Fort Clatsop

Louisiana Territory

Missouri River

Saint Louis

Spanish Territory

Arkansas River

Fort Adams

Red River

Natchitoches

N

—— Lewis & Clark
----- Lewis & Clark return
—— Pike
—— Freeman-Custis

Exploring the West

Examine the routes of the three expeditions discussed in the chapter. How are the routes different? Why are they different?

Freeman-Custis Expedition

Jefferson sent another team west. Thomas Freeman would explore the Red River. Freeman was a surveyor. His team included Peter Custis, who was a botanist, and 35 other men. They would record the wildlife of the area.

Freeman and Custis launched their expedition from Fort Adams in the Mississippi Territory on April 19, 1806. They searched for the Red River's headwaters. They were also to make alliances with local tribes. The team traveled through parts of present-day Louisiana, Oklahoma, Texas, and Arkansas. But Spanish soldiers chased the team. The Spanish caught up. They told Freeman to turn back. Freeman's team turned around on July 30. The return journey would take a month.

The team did not find the Red's headwaters. But Freeman recorded the river's route. Custis noted 267 animals and plants. And the team's meetings with tribes gave the United States more control over the land.

Meriwether Lewis made a journal entry in April 1805. He and the rest of the corps were departing Fort Mandan. They would head farther west:

> . . . *we were now about to penetrate a country at least two thousand miles [3,200 km] in width, on which the foot of civilized man had never trodden; the good or evil it had in store for us was for experiment yet to determine, and these little vessells contained every article by which we were to expect to subsist or defend ourselves.*

Source: Jay H. Buckley. "Lewis and Clark Expedition." Encyclopædia Britannica. Encyclopædia Britannica, December 15, 2014. Web. Accessed January 6, 2016.

What's the Big Idea?

Take a close look at this journal entry. What is Lewis trying to say about the expedition? Pick out two details he uses to make his point. What words stand out to you? What feelings do they convey?

CHAPTER THREE

EXPANDING WEST

Thomas Jefferson wanted the United States to expand west. He believed owning land would help create a strong nation. He thought it would make the country rich and happy. Westward expansion happened quickly after the Louisiana Purchase. Between 1790 and 1820, the US population grew from 3.9 million to 9.6 million. In 1790 only 5 percent of Americans lived west of the Appalachian

Jefferson used treaties with Native Americans to move them off their land.

Mountains. That had grown to 25 percent in 1820. Expansion helped the United States grow and prosper. But it came at a high price to many people.

Native Americans

Throughout the 1800s, Native Americans' lives changed dramatically. Jefferson promoted treaties with Native Americans. Treaties would benefit the United States. Native Americans would be bound to the United States rather than European nations. East of the Mississippi, tribes signed more than 40 treaties. Jefferson hoped treaties would make Native Americans conform to American culture. Treaties established trade agreements and gave control of tribal land to the United States. This was essential to westward expansion.

But Jefferson also fought the Native Americans. Under Jefferson, Andrew Jackson led US Army forces in battles against tribes. Eventually, the government forced thousands of Native Americans to relocate. While president from 1829 to 1837, Jackson focused on obtaining Native American land. He signed almost 70 treaties to move Native Americans to Indian Territory in present-day Oklahoma. By 1840 the United States had forced tens of thousands of Native Americans to walk there. The journey became known as the Trail of Tears. The name reflects the pain and suffering Native Americans experienced along the route. Relocating Native Americans gave the United

The US government forced many tribes off their land.

States at least 25 million acres (10 million ha) of land in the southeast.

Over the next three decades, Native Americans in the West would suffer a similar fate. Tribes there also signed treaties. They gave up their lands and ended up on reservations. Settlers also pushed Native Americans off their land. The transcontinental railroad was built on some Native American land. Railroad construction changed the environment. Workers laid permanent tracks. They felled trees for railroad ties and bridges. Native Americans relied on bison as a food source. White people hunted the bison to near extinction. Native Americans lost their land and their way of life. Meanwhile, white people sought more opportunities on the western frontier.

Slavery

The Louisiana Territory presented opportunities for another issue: the spread of slavery. The practice was common in the southern United States. It divided

Sand Creek Massacre

In the West, some Native Americans fought settlers. But some tribes were allies with the United States, including a band of Cheyenne in the Colorado Territory. Chief Black Kettle led them. The group sought refuge at Fort Lyon in the Colorado Territory. They settled along Sand Creek. US soldiers were attacking other Cheyenne tribes. The band was concerned that they would be attacked, too. The chief flew US and white flags to show no ill will to settlers. But on November 29, 1864, John Chivington led his 700 volunteer soldiers in an attack on the tribe. The troops brutally killed more than 100 Cheyenne, mostly women and children.

Americans. The debate over slavery in the West escalated in 1819. Missouri had applied for statehood. At the time, there were 22 states. Eleven allowed slavery. Eleven did not. They were free states. Missouri wanted to allow slavery. Granting Missouri statehood would tip the balance of power in the government. Free-state politicians fought this.

After much debate, the US Congress came to an agreement in 1820. The Missouri Compromise would admit Missouri as a slave state and Maine as a free state. This would balance power. Second, an imaginary line was established across the rest of the Louisiana Territory. Except for Missouri, all land north of the line would make slavery illegal. Land south of it would allow slavery.

The compromise only temporarily kept the nation from dividing. The arguments grew as the United States kept expanding west. In 1854, the Kansas-Nebraska Act nullified the Missouri Compromise. It left the slavery decision to residents

Americans against slavery organized to fight those who were for it during Bleeding Kansas.

of a territory applying for statehood. That year, Kansas and Nebraska became territories. Slavery in both was left to popular vote. Slavery was not an issue in Nebraska. The people living there were from the Midwest, a free area. But slavery was a major topic for Kansas. Many residents were opposed to slavery. But their neighbors in Missouri were in favor of it. People on both sides of the issue rushed to the state to influence the vote. Violence erupted in 1855 and 1856. Kansas fought a civil war. Hundreds of people died. The war is known as Bleeding Kansas.

Kansas entered the Union as a free state in 1861. But debate over slavery continued. It became even more heated. That same year, the American Civil War (1861–1865) began over slavery. Westward expansion had triggered the deadliest war in US history. More than 620,000 Americans would die. Millions more would be injured. But the war would free all slaves in America.

Andrew Jackson gave his second annual address to Congress on December 6, 1830. He spoke about removing Native Americans from their lands. He said:

> *The removal of the Indians beyond the white settlements is approaching to a happy consummation. . . . The consequences of a speedy removal will be important to the United States, to individual States, and to the Indians themselves. . . . It will separate the Indians from immediate contact with settlements of whites . . . and perhaps cause them gradually, under the protection of the Government and through the influence of good counsels, to cast off their savage habits and become an interesting, civilized, and Christian community.*

Source: "Andrew Jackson's Second Annual Message." Africans in America. Twin Cities Public Television, n.d. Web. Accessed January 27, 2016.

Changing Minds

This passage discusses removing Native Americans from their lands to make way for US expansion west. Imagine you are living in 1830. Take a position against removing Native Americans from their lands. Write a short essay trying to change the minds of others from the 1830s. Make sure you detail your opinion and your reasons for it. Include facts and details that support your reasons.

CHAPTER FOUR

CHANGING A NATION

The United States paid off the loan for the Louisiana Purchase in 1823. With 6 percent interest, the final cost was more than $23.5 million. That was a few cents per acre. The purchase was perhaps the greatest real estate deal in history. It was also a turning point for the United States, France, and Spain.

The Louisiana Purchase shifted the balance of power in North America.

Giving the territory to France weakened Spain's New World presence. Then Napoléon abandoned his goal to create an empire in the region. After selling the territory to the United States, France would no longer play a major role in North America. Doubling the United States' land mass provided new opportunities for growth. Americans took advantage of the territory's resources. They had more farmland. They could use the Mississippi River freely. Meanwhile Spain was weakening further. By 1819 the once-powerful nation would give up the last of its territories to the United States.

Gumbo Stew

The area that became the state of Louisiana was home to a variety of people. In 1803, residents were Native Americans, free blacks, slaves, and people of French ancestry. During the next ten years, around 10,000 refugees from the Caribbean joined the mix. They were a combination of black and white people. Some were free. Some were slaves. This diversity is still visible today. The New Orleans stew called gumbo takes ingredients from French, Native American, and West African foods, among other cultures.

For Thomas Jefferson, the Louisiana Purchase led to success in exploration and expansion. The purchase also helped him get reelected. It had created a sense of American nationalism. But for thousands of other people, the purchase had disastrous results.

Native Americans after Westward Expansion

Westward expansion forever changed Native Americans' traditional way of life. The US government and white settlers took their lands. Today, there are still tensions between Native Americans and the US government. Native American tribes can live on about 56 million acres (23 million ha) of land the United States has reserved for them. About 325 federal reservations existed in 2015. Tribes can become federally recognized. Federally recognized tribes are self-governing. They deal with the United States as one government to another. In 2015, the US government changed the rules for gaining recognition in an attempt to make it easier.

Tribes work with the United States as one government to another.

But Native Americans still face challenges. Economic struggles burden many. The poverty rate for Native Americans is double that of the entire US population. Unemployment rates on some reservations have been as high as 81 percent.

And many Native Americans ponder questions about identity and culture. During westward expansion, the US government pushed white culture on Native Americans. They encouraged tribes to give up their traditions and assimilate into white society. That pressure remains today. Many tribes have lost parts of their culture, including language. Up to 300 Native American languages have been forgotten since Europeans began arriving in America. Some tribes are restoring their native tongues. The Tongva tribe in California is using old recordings and records to reconstruct their language. Learning their ancestors' language

PERSPECTIVES
Lewis and Clark's Legacy

Reenactors followed Lewis and Clark's trail on the expedition's 200th anniversary. People cheered the reenactors' progress. The trek was easier than Lewis and Clark's. Reenactors had boats with motors. They had clean drinking water. But they still dealt with ticks and mosquitoes. River debris could still harm their boats. They hoped to educate people about the trek. Some Native Americans protested the reenactment in South Dakota. They wanted reenactors to consider how the expedition enabled white people to forever change Native Americans' way of life.

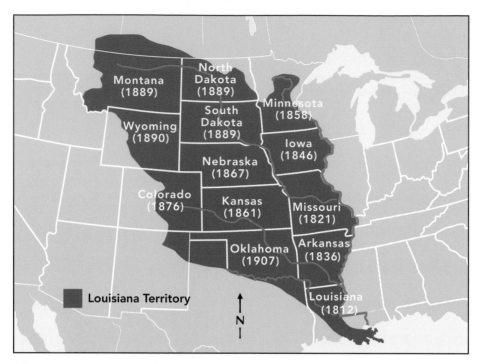

The Territory Today
The Louisiana Territory was gradually split into many states. This map shows each state made from the territory and the year it became a state. Why do you think the territory was divided?

can help a tribe unite its members, keep its identity, and honor its history.

The Land Two Centuries Later

Today, the land of the Louisiana Purchase has several names. Louisiana became the first state carved from the territory. It achieved statehood on April 30, 1812. That was the ninth anniversary of the historic agreement made with France. Fourteen other states' borders were later drawn from the territory.

The Louisiana Territory launched Americans into the West. The West would help define the nation during the 1800s. It gave the country room to grow and become self-sustaining. This set up the United States to become a powerful country. The surprise sale made history. It made the United States what it is today.

EXPLORE ONLINE

The website below has even more information about the Louisiana Purchase. But every source is different. Reread Chapter Four of this book. What are the similarities between it and the information you found on the website? Are there any differences? How do the two sources present information differently?

Louisiana Purchase
mycorelibrary.com/louisiana-purchase

KEY LOCATIONS

Modern US borders

5

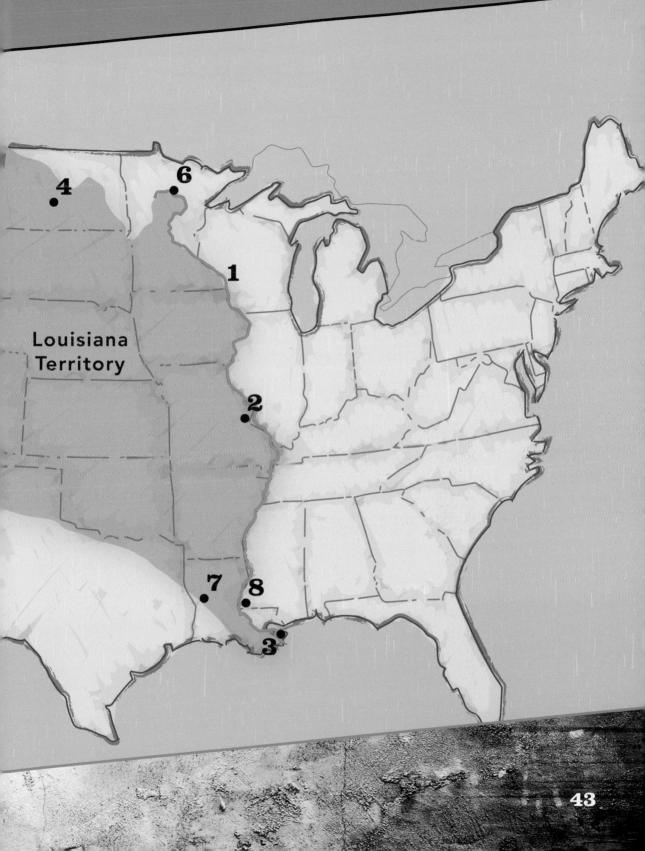

Louisiana
Territory

4

6

1

2

7 8

3

STOP AND THINK

You Are There

This book discusses the Corps of Discovery's interactions with Native Americans. Imagine you are a member of a tribe visited by the Corps of Discovery. What do you think of the presentations the Corps gives? What do you think about their intentions?

Tell the Tale

Chapter Two of this book discusses some of the expeditions of the West following the Louisiana Purchase. Write 200 words that tell the story of Meriwether Lewis and William Clark. What were the goals of their expedition? Was it successful? Be sure to set the scene, develop a sequence of events, and offer a conclusion.

Surprise Me

Chapter Three discusses some of the results of the United States buying the Louisiana Territory from France. After reading this book, what two or three facts about acquiring that land did you find most surprising? Write a few sentences about each fact. Why did you find them surprising?

Say What?

Studying history means learning a lot of new vocabulary. Find five words in this book that you have never heard before. Use a dictionary to find out what they mean. Next, write the meanings in your own words, and use each word in a new sentence.

GLOSSARY

alliances
agreements when two or
more groups of people join
together for a common cause

botanist
someone who studies plants

expedition
a group of people who take a
trip to explore an area

nationalism
feeling loyal to a country,
believing that the country is
better than others

negotiate
to work out an agreement by
talking about it

northwest passage
a hoped-for water route
through the northwest part of
North America

trading posts
remote places used to
exchange goods for other
goods or money

transcontinental
going across a continent

treaty
an agreement made by
negotiation

tribes
groups of people who have
the same language, customs,
beliefs, and often the same
ancestors

LEARN MORE

Books

Fradin, Dennis B. *The Louisiana Purchase*. Tarrytown, NY: Marshall Cavendish Benchmark Books, 2010.

Rea, Amy C. *The Trail of Tears*. Minneapolis, MN: Abdo Publishing, 2016.

St. George, Judith. *What Was the Lewis and Clark Expedition?* New York: Grosset & Dunlap, 2014.

Websites

To learn more about the Wild West, visit **booklinks.abdopublishing.com**. These links are routinely monitored and updated to provide the most current information available.

Visit **mycorelibrary.com** for free additional tools for teachers and students.

INDEX

ABOUT THE AUTHOR

Rebecca Rowell has used her publishing and writing degree to edit and write many books for Abdo Publishing. Her recent books include topics on ancient India, the US Marine Corps, and Sylvia Earle. She lives in Minneapolis, Minnesota.